GOD, WHY ME?

God, Why Me?

Erwin W. Lutzer

Moody Church Media
Chicago

Cover by Bryan Butler

GOD, WHY ME?
Copyright © 2022 by Erwin W. Lutzer
Published by Moody Church Media
Chicago, Illinois 60614
www.moodymedia.org

ISBN: 9798357471550

CONTENTS

CHAPTER 1

GOD, WHY ME?

A young man said goodbye to his family and friends and boarded a plane that would take him to a faraway country as a missionary. En route, the plane had an intermediate stop, so he tore a piece of paper from a newspaper, scribbled a note, and mailed it home; then he resumed his journey.

Unfortunately, the plane crashed and he was killed along with all others aboard. His parents were devastated by the news and a few days later, received the note he had written at the airport. According to the story, they read the note, then flipped the scrap of paper to the other side. There, printed in thick dark newsprint, was the short three-letter word, WHY?

Suffering comes in so many different forms. For some it's the dreaded news from a doctor's report. For others it's the death of a spouse or child, the breakup of a marriage, or the heartache caused by a delinquent son or daughter. Others have financial reversals, unjust accusations, and accidents of every kind.

The book of Job is a poetic drama that speaks directly to these circumstances. It is a literary masterpiece with a wealth of insight into the human dilemma of a life wrenched by unexpected grief and emotional turbulence. Here we have a window into the ways of God in the world. This story of high drama in the heavenlies helps us interpret the painful, often haphazard experiences of our lives on Earth.

This book is generally believed to be one of the oldest in the Bible. Since it makes no reference to institutions such as the priesthood, scholars generally date it before Abraham, Isaac, and Jacob. The archaic Hebrew expressions also give testimony to its ancient origin.

Job, though limited in his knowledge of God, was a good man who turned away from evil. "There was a man in the land of Uz whose name was Job, and that man was blameless and upright, one who feared God and turned away from evil" (Job 1:1). He was also wealthy, with seven sons, three daughters, and possessions that were the envy of his friends.

But his idyllic life was about to change. Everything he considered dear would be torn from him. His children, his health, and his stature in the community would soon vanish. He would even have reason to question the commitment of his own distraught wife. He was about to embark on a life that would be directly opposite to what he had known. And it would happen in a single day.

Let's plunge into the story by considering the three personalities involved in this made-for-viewing drama. We'll be surprised at how God, the devil, and Job all have a role to play as the scenes unfold.

The curtain opens with God on center stage. He, after all, is the prime mover behind the events of life. Job's trial begins with God's permission and ends with a breathtaking revelation from the Almighty Himself. And what happens between scene one and the final act rivets our attention.

GOD'S ROLE IN JOB'S SUFFERING

Satan and his cohorts show up in the presence of God for what appears to be a daily briefing. "Have you considered my servant Job?" (Job 1:8), God asks Satan, appearing eager to talk about His special trophy. God, we notice, is the one who initiates the encounter.

Satan has a ready reply. "Does Job fear God for no reason? Have you not put a hedge around him and his house and all that he has, on every side? You have blessed the work of his hands, and his possessions have increased in the land. But stretch out your hand and touch all that he has, and he will curse you to your face" (Job 1:9–11). Satan is basically saying: Of course Job serves God, because the Almighty has been so good to him!

God picks up the gauntlet hurled down by the tempter.

He gives Satan permission to strip Job of everything precious to him. But there is a limit: Satan cannot touch Job's body. God remains in control even though Satan is given the coveted powers of wreaking havoc on Job and his family. Satan knows he must always be subject to God. He cannot overstep the parameters ordered by the Almighty.

God had, in effect, taunted Satan about His righteous child, Job. And now that He has given the evil one authority to search and destroy, we wait on the sidelines, wondering what will befall this good man.

This suffering originated within the plans and purposes of God. But though God is about to throw Job into the furnace of affliction, His hand will still be on the thermostat. God does not stand on the sidelines but is an active player in the plight of His choice servant.

SATAN'S ROLE IN JOB'S SUFFERING

God *controls* the extent of the suffering, but Satan *implements* it. We marvel at the power God has given him to direct evil marauders and even control the elements of nature. Job is sitting in his tent reflecting on his blessings when four messengers come running toward him, one after another bringing dire news.

The first reported that a band of Sabeans attacked Job's servants, killing them along with his donkeys and oxen. The messenger had seen it with his own eyes, and ends by saying, "...and I alone have escaped to tell you" (Job 1:15).

The words were scarcely out of his mouth when another servant breathlessly reported that lightning had struck the servants who were caring for Job's sheep. The sheep and the servants were dead; he ends with the same words, "...and I alone have escaped to tell you" (1:16).

The words have not yet sunk into Job's heart when a third messenger reported that the Chaldeans formed three bands and stole Job's camels and killed the servants who cared for them. Again Job hears the familiar words, "and I alone have escaped to tell you" (1:17).

Job was devastated, but there was worse to come. Another servant came with the most terrible news of all. "Your sons and daughters were eating and drinking wine in their oldest brother's house, and behold, a great wind came across the wilderness and struck the four corners of the house, and it fell upon the young people, and they are dead, and I alone have escaped to tell you" (Job 1:18–19).

Even the power of death is in Satan's hands!

If your name were Job, what conclusions would you draw about God and your relationship to Him? Or to put it another way, was Job's calamity from God or the devil? The answer is that it was from *both*—God and the devil. God didn't personally bring the wind and the lightning, but because He allowed Satan to do it, Job could look at this tragedy as coming from the Almighty. Satan is the *immediate* cause of Job's suffering; God is the *ultimate* cause of it.

Job understood that his calamity was from God. He knew that marauders, lightning, and wind were responsible for his misfortune, but all of these causes were in God's hands. "The LORD gave, and the LORD has taken away; blessed be the name of the LORD" (Job 1:21).

We can say that cancer took the life of a Christian. But when we think about it, it was God who allowed the disease to spread; it was God who chose not to heal the person after the disease entered the body. Cancer is the immediate cause. God is the one who stands in back of what happened as the ultimate cause.

Of course, many people think it's unwise to speak so candidly about God's role in human suffering. I've had people say, "If you tell parents that God took their child, they'll be angry with Him." Some people think it's better to place all responsibility on the immediate cause such as cancer, a tornado, or an accident, than the ultimate cause, God.

But at the end of the book, we are told that Job's brothers and sisters came to comfort him, "for all the evil that the LORD had brought upon him" (Job 42:11). He looked past the immediate causes and saw that his grief was given to him by God.

Of course, we should never *blame* God, since the word

implies that someone acted irresponsibly. But to say that our suffering comes from God, to say that God permitted what happened, and thus could have chosen to not permit it, is simply to affirm God's sovereignty in the affairs of men. Even Satan has all the limitations of a creature and thus can only act with God's express permission and consent.

JOB'S ROLE IN HIS SUFFERING

At this point, Job was a model sufferer. He fell to the ground, worshiped, and affirmed God's right to give and take. "Then Job arose and tore his robe and shaved his head and fell on the ground and worshiped. And he said, 'Naked I came from my mother's womb, and naked shall I return. The LORD gave, and the LORD has taken away; blessed be the name of the LORD.' In all this Job did not sin or charge God with wrong" (Job 1:20–22).

It doesn't occur to him to curse the wind, the lightning, the Sabeans, or the Chaldeans. Most important, he does not curse God. Instead, he affirms God's right to do as He wishes.

When his wife suggests that he curse God and die, Job refuses her advice, however sincerely it was offered. "You speak as one of the foolish women would speak. Shall we receive good from God, and shall we not receive evil?" (Job 2:10). God was good when things were going well, and God was still good even though things were going badly. If we accept good, we should also accept adversity.

Actually, the Hebrew word is normally translated as "bless," but given the context, most translations agree that "curse" is the meaning we should attribute to it here. Whether we curse God or bless Him depends on our disposition. We will respond according to the measure of our faith. At this point, Job has passed the test admirably.

Now we must back off and consider some life-changing lessons that jump from the pages of this cosmic drama. Perhaps we will never view our own trials quite the same again.

LIFE-CHANGING LESSONS

First, *every trial is a test to see how much God means to us*. We need to ask ourselves: Is God worthy of worship apart from the blessings He gives us? Or do we serve Him only because it's profitable to do so?

Let's revisit Satan's reply to God, "Does Job fear God for no reason? Have you not put a hedge around him...?" The devil is saying, "You are buying Job's worship and allegiance! He's serving You because of the blessings You've given him! Anyone would serve You if You gave them a fine family and wealth!"

The accusation is that Job is serving God because he'd been bribed. Take away his perks and he will curse God. We face the same challenge almost every day. Do we serve God only when He gives us blessings? Is God good only when life goes our way? Or is God good even when our children are killed in a windstorm or murdered by an intruder?

One summer when we returned from vacation, I said to our children, "God was so good in protecting us from an accident or mechanical failure with our car." The moment the words were out of my mouth, I felt a rebuke in my spirit. Would God not be good if we had a flat tire, an overheated radiator, or an accident?

So we come full circle. Do we worship God for the benefits we receive, or is God worthy of our devotion even when there is no evidence of His blessing? Do we worship God for what we can get out of Him? Must we be bribed into our commitment?

Second, *when God wishes to test a person, nothing is untouchable!* We are startled to discover that Satan was given the power to have Job's ten children killed. Think of these ten young lives with a future ahead of them. Ten lives with the potential of enjoyment and blessing. And now there were ten fresh graves on the side of the hill. Looked at in one way, it appeared as if the children were expendable. And because God wanted to try Job, they were expendable!

God does not have to give us healthy families, fine homes, and happy times. He has the right to give children and to take them; to keep us from sickness and to let us suffer. When He really wants to test the depth of our allegiance, He takes that which is closest to our hearts.

A third lesson is that *events on Earth must be interpreted in light of events in heaven.* Think this through: Job didn't know that God and the devil had this dialogue about him. He was not privy to the challenge that Satan laid before God somewhere in the heavenlies. If he had known he was being watched by angels, demons, and God, if he had known he was a test case, he could have endured the trial much more easily.

Perhaps God and the devil have had a dialogue about you recently. You and I might be chosen for an unexpected test that will reverse our fortunes. Yes, we are being watched in the heavenlies. Whether we pass or fail the test is more important in heaven than it is on Earth.

Finally, Job reminds us that *it is possible to worship God even if we have unanswered questions.* Job didn't have any warning for this trial; he received no revelation regarding its purposes. After the bad news, he received no memo giving a rationale for what happened. The tragedy began suddenly, with no warning and no opportunity for recourse.

With his heart pounding with grief, Job fell on his face and worshiped. He did not curse God, nor did he demand an explanation. He accepted God's right to give and to take.

We all know people who will die with unanswered questions. A couple whose son's death was ruled a suicide is convinced he was actually murdered. Another couple whose child was found dead in a ditch has no explanation for what happened.

At a conference, a man said to me, "My son committed suicide…if he is not in heaven, I don't want to go there myself…I would rather be in hell." Perhaps his son is in heaven, I trust it is so. Meanwhile, this distraught father must learn to worship God without knowing his child's fate. He must believe that whatever God does, He indeed has the right to do.

This distraught father must even conclude that if his son is in hell, God is still worthy of worship. We do not need an explanation; we do need Someone we can trust. God alone can fill that role.

We will all have to wait until we get to heaven to find out the whys and the wherefores. And yet, bless them, many have not abandoned their faith in God though His purposes are obscure.

> I walked a mile with Pleasure;
> She chattered all the way,
> But left me none the wiser
> For all she had to say.
>
> I walked a mile with Sorrow
> And ne'er a word said she;

But oh, the things I learned from her
When Sorrow walked with me!
        —"Along the Road"
            by Robert Browning Hamilton

Job started well, but the sorrow began to wear on him.
God turned up the heat, and the heavens remained silent.

CHAPTER 2

GOD, I'VE LOST EVERYTHING

Suffering increases our perplexity. Our conviction that God is loving is of small comfort when our lives become unraveled. If He loves us, we wonder, why does He expect us to endure such misfortune? Love, we think, means that we should be kept from tears rather than having them wiped from our face. Suffering makes us rethink our understanding of God. We thought we knew God, but now we must conclude that we cannot fathom Him. Senseless grief brings unsettled doubt.

A young missionary is killed in a freak car accident, leaving a wife and children behind. God wants people to hear the gospel, yet allows one of His servants to be under a car when the jack gives way. A Christian mother dies in childbirth leaving her husband alone to raise the baby. A child is gunned down in a random shooting on a Chicago street. Add to this, seemingly lesser trials—injustice in the workplace, a disabled child, and an adulterous marriage.

Let's walk through the life of Job with a video camera, asking him what he was thinking during the good times as well as the bad. Let us observe his emotional and spiritual temperature. And let us find out what he truly believed about God.

SCENE ONE: JOB HAS EVERYTHING

Prior to that fateful day, if Job had been living in our time, he would have been invited to talk shows to share his secret of success. He was blessed, he might have argued, because of his faithfulness toward God. He would have said that if you walk rightly and trust God, He will make you healthy, wealthy, and wise. If you are a child of royalty, why not live like one?

"Follow the Lord," Job might have said, "and you'll never have to cry yourself to sleep. Your children will be models of character and will make wise choices about their careers and marriage partners." Life for the people of faith, life for the committed, is facing one challenge after another successfully. Doors of opportunity open and all we have to do is walk through them by faith. The righteous find their paths graced with little flowers as they walk in the sunshine enjoying the cool breezes.

That might have been Job's speech during those heady days of prosperity, but his tune changed. No more talk about prosperity as the inheritance of the obedient. No more condemnation of the poor, chiding them for their lack of faith and failure to follow the Lord.

The days of blessing were wonderful as long as they lasted, but now they were but a dim memory. The man who had everything now had nothing. Job was reduced to the same existence as his neighbors down the street, except that he was poorer and in more pain.

SCENE TWO: JOB HAS NOTHING

After Satan was granted his first liberty, Job lost his livestock, servants, and his beloved children. But at this point, his health was still intact. God had told Satan he could do as he wished, but he could not touch Job's body.

Job and his wife are still grieving as another storm looms on the horizon. In the heavenly realms, another discussion is taking place. God again brings up the subject of Job and provides an update on his progress. "Have you considered my servant Job, that there is none like him on the earth, a blameless and upright man, who fears God and turns away from evil? He still holds fast his integrity, although you incited me against him to destroy him without reason" (Job 2:3).

Job was being destroyed "without reason!" Of course, God had a reason, but so far as Job was concerned there was no rational cause for his tragedy. The news came to him swiftly and without explanation. Such tragedies were known to happen only to the wicked. Because he was righteous, Job was baffled.

Satan responds as we might predict, "Skin for skin! All that a man has he will give for his life. But stretch out your hand and touch his bone and his flesh, and he will curse you to your face" (2:4–5). With Job in robust health, God was still worthy of worship. But, said Satan, if you touch him personally, he will give up his allegiance. He can endure the fate of his children, but he cannot endure personal pain and humiliation.

Again, God gives Satan the right to do as he wills except that Job's life must be spared. Apart from that, any physical debilitation Satan wants to inflict is fair game. With glee, Satan immediately leaves the presence of the Lord and smites Job with sores "from the sole of his foot to the crown of his head" (2:7).

Pain shoots through Job's body as the boils break out, causing lesions and severe itching. In desperation, he takes a broken piece of pottery and scrapes himself while sitting in the ash heap. He is destitute and foreboding, seeking some word of encouragement, some assurance that God has not abandoned him.

Job's wife now enters the picture and says, "Do you still hold fast your integrity? Curse God and die" (2:9). No doubt she suggested this because she loved Job and did not want to see him suffer. Without realizing it, she was repeating the exact words of Satan; it was he who had predicted that if Job were reduced to poverty and illness, he would curse God. Though she might have meant well, Job pointedly rejected her suggestion.

"You speak as one of the foolish women would speak. Shall we receive good from God, and shall we not receive evil?" (2:10). At this point, Job held his tongue, refusing to speak against God. He will eventually come close to cursing God, but not now.

Each year, 45,000 Americans are so convinced that death is preferable to life that they commit suicide. And although Job will wish that he had never been born and will long for death, he never takes that irrevocable step. If Job had died here, think of all that he would have missed. Think also of what we would have missed. He would have faded from the pages of history like other mortals, and certainly we would not be learning from him today. Suicide is never an answer to our perplexity and pain. We should not jump off the boat; we should trust God's timing to bring us to the harbor.

Job is reduced to sitting on a heap of ashes, scratching his sores. Few people in life have less than he. Still grieving over the death of his precious children, he finds scant comfort from his wife. Now he has little to do but contemplate his fate and wonder what happened to the God he thought he knew.

Because Job was well known, three friends came from a great distance to sit with him to interpret his predicament. They sit on the edge of the ash heap, listening to his grief. They will have plenty of time to speak later; indeed, they shall speak far too much. For now they hear his soliloquy of despair.

SCENE THREE: JOB FALLS INTO DESPAIR

Though Job initially accepted his fate with confidence in God, he began to lose heart. Those who have had a long hospital stay tell us that keeping a positive attitude is possible for the first few days, but depression will soon settle upon the soul. God can often be seen at the beginning of a tragedy, but as the weariness settles in, it's more difficult to see His hand.

Job's faith slips. He longs for death; his initial burst of praise has turned toward perplexity. He thought he had God figured out; he believed he knew where he stood with the Almighty, but now he isn't sure. The foundation of his faith had taken a direct hit. He was face to face with a God he didn't know. He went from the sunlight into a dark tunnel of doubt and emotional numbness.

If you believe that blessing comes by serving God, Job could no longer be blessed, for his service for God had ended. He had nothing left to offer, no works to perform, no acts of charity to bestow. Like a disabled person in a retirement home, Job had nothing to contribute to the welfare of others. Instead of serving, he would have to be served.

Job does not curse God, but he does curse the day of his birth. "Let the day perish on which I was born, and the night that said, 'A man is conceived.' Let that day be darkness! May God above not seek it, nor light shine upon it. Let gloom and deep darkness claim it. Let clouds dwell upon it; let the blackness of the day terrify it" (Job 3:3–5).

So he continues, wishing he had never been born, wishing his mother had miscarried, for "There the wicked cease from troubling, and there the weary are at rest" (3:17). Job questions why a person is born if all that he experiences is suffering. He is overwhelmed by the pointlessness of it all.

Job does not realize that one day we would study his experience to draw lessons that would help us understand God's ways with His people. For us, though not for him, glimmers of light are shining through. Again we pause to grasp what we have learned so far.

POWERFUL LESSONS

First, *the best believers are often the most sorely tempted.* Job was not laid waste because he was an evil man but because he was a good man. In fact, the trial came right after Job had renewed his commitment to God. Bad things do happen to good people.

When Jesus walked by a blind man, He said that the

blindness had happened not because of the man's sin, nor the sin of his parents, but rather that "...the works of God might be displayed in him" (John 9:3). You cannot look at a person's economic or medical status and deduce where he is spiritually. There is often no clear cause–effect relationship between a righteous life and health and wealth.

What we do know is that our faith is most precious to God; and that, in itself, is an explanation for the seemingly random suffering of life. If we can believe that God is good even when He seems to be working against us, such faith is to the honor and praise of God.

Second, *prosperity and pain come from the same hand.* Job, as we've learned, was initially comforted with the knowledge that we are to receive both good and adversity from the hand of the Lord. If he had taken his own words more seriously, he could have managed his suffering much better.

There's a story about a Chinese man who had a son and a horse. When the horse ran away, the neighbors came to comfort their friend regarding the evil that had befallen him.

"How do you know that this is evil?" asked the man.

The next day, the horse returned and brought seven stray horses with him. So the friends now returned to rejoice with the man for the good that had befallen him.

"How do you know that this is good?" the man now asked.

The next day, his son was thrown from one of the stray

horses and broke his leg. So the neighbors gathered again to comfort the man regarding the evil that had befallen him.

"How do you know that this is evil?" he asked.

The next day, soldiers came through the countryside looking for young men to be conscripted for battle. His son, now incapacitated, was exempt. The neighbors gathered once more to rejoice with their friend regarding this good twist of fortune.

"How do you know that this is good?" he asked.

The point, of course, is that we, as Christians, do not make superficial judgments regarding what is good and evil. We who live on this side of the cross know that everything comes to us from the nail-pierced hands of Christ. Indeed, "...all things work together for good..." (Romans 8:28). We might be having a terrible day, but actually, it is a very good day! God makes it come out for our benefit.

Finally, let us remember that *God is with us in our depression and doubt.* Though Job does not yet know it, the Lord heard his cry from the ash heap. God was not unmindful of Job's mental and spiritual darkness. There was a reason why he didn't die at birth.

If only Job had known the beginning and the end of his own life story, he would have found his sores more bearable. But for now, he copes as best he can, hoping for a word of comfort from his friends.

They want to help, but they hurt.

ERWIN W. LUTZER

CHAPTER 3

WHEN COMFORT IS DISCOMFORT

There is a story, perhaps fictitious, of a young seminarian in training for church ministry. A requirement was that he receive experience in hospital visitation. He was nervous but confident as he walked onto the floor and began his rounds as chaplain.

While whispering Scripture verses into the ear of a man hooked up to a series of tubes, the young man noticed the patient becoming extremely agitated. The sick man furiously motioned with his hands, asking for a pencil and a piece of paper. When his request was granted, he scrawled a note, and then immediately expired.

The seminarian was aghast at what had happened before his very eyes. He called the nurses and soon the body of the patient was taken away. Only later did the young minister read the note the dying man had written: "You are standing on my oxygen tube!"

We smile, of course, but I'm sure we all have friends who

intended to help us but ended up doing more harm than good. Or at least we can say that their supposed comfort turned out to be discomfort. Words that were supposed to help turned out to hurt.

Job had three friends who were good men, but they approached Job's suffering in the wrong way. Some of their advice was good, some of it was bad, and some of it was irrelevant. They gave long speeches that were intended to shed light on their friend's predicament; but when they were finished, he was left in greater darkness.

If you have read the book of Job, you will have noticed that each man speaks three times (except Zophar who speaks twice, then later in the book, a young man takes his place for the third round). Job replies to each of these speeches, making the book very lengthy. At the end God enters and responds to Job directly.

In this study, I will not comment on each of the speeches, but give a basic summary of what these counselors had to say. More important for us, we will discover why God was so displeased with their advice and insights. In the process, we will better understand how to comfort those who mourn.

ELIPHAZ THE TEMANITE

Eliphaz was polite but critical of Job, basing his teaching on a mystical experience in which he purported to receive a revelation from God. He doesn't give Job much hope. "Remember: who that was innocent ever perished? Or where were the upright cut off? As I have seen, those who plow iniquity and sow trouble reap the same" (Job 4:7–8).

Job replies by pouring out his vexation, grief, and anguish. "Oh that my vexation were weighed, and all my calamity laid in the balances! For then it would be heavier than the sand of the sea; therefore my words have been rash. For the arrows of the Almighty are in me; my spirit drinks their poison; the terrors of God are arrayed against me" (Job 6:2–4).

Job feels put upon. All he heard was self-righteous condemnation. His wound becomes deeper, the pain more intense. Eliphaz will have more to say later, but his tone will not get better. If anything, he will be more belligerent.

Not much sympathy here.

BILDAD THE SHUHITE

"Just seek God, Job!"

That, in summary, was the message of Bildad. "If you will seek God and plead with the Almighty for mercy, if you are pure and upright, surely then he will rouse himself for you and restore your rightful habitation" (Job 8:5–6). God, he says, is giving you what you deserve. Tradition gives us insight and it pronounces you guilty.

Job reacts by saying in effect, "Okay, suppose you are

right, how do I go about finding God?" Words are cheap. "Truly I know that it is so: But how can a man be in the right before God?" (9:2). Bildad's rebuke only makes Job sink deeper into despair because he cannot find God no matter where he turns. Just listen to his grief:

"Why did you bring me out from the womb? Would that I had died before any eye had seen me and were as though I had not been, carried from the womb to the grave" (10:18–19). He contemplates death, and hopes that when it comes, he will never return. He longs for darkness and oblivion.

Bildad will have more to say, much more. Like a broken record, he will rehearse Job's failures and urge him to turn to God. Job believes he has already done so, but Bildad will disagree, spouting platitudes.

Some comfort.

ZOPHAR THE NAAMATHITE

Job's third friend seems to be the meanest of them all. "Should a multitude of words go unanswered, and a man full of talk be judged right?" (Job 11:2). He accuses Job of arrogance and falsehood. God, he says, "knows worthless men; when he sees iniquity, will he not consider it?" (11:11). Just get honest and admit your sin!

Job turns angry and sarcastic. "No doubt you are the people, and wisdom will die with you. But I have understanding as well as you; I am not inferior to you. Who does not know such things as these?" (12:2–3). He gives a lengthy, bitter reply, calling his friends "worthless physicians" (13:4) who should remain silent. His disappointment is more than he can bear.

What did God think of these three friends? God was even more displeased with their conduct than Job was. At the end of the book, the Almighty gives His verdict. "After the LORD had spoken these words to Job, the LORD said to Eliphaz the Temanite: 'My anger burns against you and against your two friends, for you have not spoken of me what is right, as my servant Job has'" (Job 42:7). In fact, Job is asked to make a burnt offering for them so that the anger of God might be appeased!

These men were counselors; they were people who claimed to have wisdom. Job called them "miserable comforters" (16:2). And God asked Job to intervene that they might not be severely disciplined.

MISTAKES THE COUNSELORS MADE

Giving wrong advice is serious business. God did not overlook their warped theology. Those who claim to speak on behalf of God had better beware.

They Talked Without Feeling

These men were having a speculative discussion about

Job's pain. Preconceived answers rolled from their lips with an air of finality and conviction. This was, for them, an opportunity to display their theological wisdom and show off their keen insights.

They could afford to be overconfident because they weren't the ones who were suffering. The iron had not pierced their own hearts. Their words made for an intellectual discussion, but not a compassionate one. It's difficult to heal a broken heart with a full head.

Read their speeches and prejudice jumps out at every turn. They had made up their minds that Job was suffering because he was guilty, and nothing could dissuade them. They made little progress in their long discourses. They just wanted Job to agree with them—the sooner the better.

Having taught theology, it's inevitable that we discuss questions such as: Do babies go to heaven when they die? We can speculate based on bits and pieces of scriptural information. But suddenly a hand is raised, and a mother says, "I had a four-year-old boy who was killed...is he in heaven?" Immediately, the atmosphere of the classroom is changed. Now the question is no longer academic; it is a question that tugs at the heart and soul.

Is it possible for a Christian to commit suicide? And if so, will he or she be in heaven? Again, it's an academic question until it is your child, your father, or your spouse who has died by a self-inflicted wound. I can still see the pain on the face of a man whose wife took her own life. Now we are talking about real people in real pain.

Those who have experienced the death of a spouse will often tell you that glib comments at funerals, even if true, often hurt deeply. "Well, he's better off now!" a friend tells the grieving widow. Of course, if the man was a believer in Christ, it is true. But if such comments are given without feeling the depth of the new widow's pain, it hurts more than it helps.

In our distress, we not only want the right answers, we want to believe that the depth of our sorrow was understood. Theoretical discussions have their place, but not for the person writhing in pain on an ash heap.

They Talked Without Listening

Read these speeches and you will discover that Job often asked questions which his friends ignored. As we have learned, they were more interested in giving their speeches than listening to his painful cries. They were not trying to see life from his point of view. There is an old adage, "Don't criticize a man until you have walked a mile in his shoes."

We've all had heart-felt discussions with people with whom we did not "connect." We said the right words and even attempted to identify with the matter at hand. But, like Job's friends, what was missing was a genuine attempt to hear what the other person was saying. That barrier

ERWIN W. LUTZER

prevented comfort from reaching the soul.

This lack of compassionate listening, however, was not the worst offense. What made God angry were the answers that the friends spit into Job's face. It was not just a lack of courtesy, but a lack of understanding that misled Job's friends. They were wrong about God. Job thought he didn't know God, but he knew Him better than his friends who purported to speak on His behalf.

They Talked Without Knowledge

Job's friends were wise, but they weren't wise enough.

They didn't know the past; they didn't know that God and the devil had a discussion about Job. They didn't know that Job had been singled out as God's showpiece. They were not privy to what was happening in the heavenlies. They assumed they knew, but they were wrong.

Nor did they know the future. They didn't know that someday Job would be restored and they would incur the wrath of the Almighty. The surprise—that the tables would be turned and Job would pray for them that they might not be judged—still awaited them.

They didn't know God's hidden plans. They had no idea that He was preparing Job for something bigger; they couldn't foresee God's ultimate intentions. They thought only in terms of a narrow cause-effect relationship. If you are righteous, God will bless you; if you are unrighteous, expect heartache. And when it comes, repent!

One day while walking along a street, I picked up bits and pieces of a letter that had been torn to shreds and scattered in the wind. I found a word here, a phrase there, but I didn't have enough pieces to make sense of the whole. So it is with God's purposes: We see an inkling here and an insight there, but the totality of the picture is hidden from us.

How would you like to have one of Job's friends visit you in a hospital? I've heard stories of sick people receiving books (often with passages underlined with a marker) that said, in effect, "If you just had enough faith, you would be healed."

Cruel.

These well-intentioned servants of God wound their friends; they do not help them. How different it would be if they were the ones who were suffering! Even faith healers have been known to change their theology when they are not healed!

Blessed are those counselors who can accept the hiddenness of God's purposes. There are matters we shall simply never understand in this world; nothing is gained by thinking we can read God's diary. Better to approach suffering with humility than overwrought confidence.

Yet God will use this bad advice in Job's life. His grief will drive him to more ultimate questions, and in the end, he will be blessed. But for now, the tunnel remains dark and foreboding.

Eventually, God will come...but not yet.

CHAPTER 4

THE SIGHS OF
A SUFFERING SOUL

No one is immune from feeling abandoned by God. Even those who write books on "How To Be Happy" experience times when there is no happiness. When multiple tragedies strike us, it's difficult to be optimistic.

Job knew the sighs of a grieving soul. We shall consider four of his soliloquies to better feel the depth of his pain and loss. Let us join him as he gropes for God but finds only frustration and abandonment.

He struggles to reconcile two great facts that clash in his mind: God's goodness and God's power.

THE SIGH OF DEPRESSION—
LONGING FOR DEATH

Again Job contemplates how much better it would have been if he had never been born; and if born, to have died at birth. Whatever darkness the dying infant might experience, it cannot be as terrible as the grief of a suffering adult.

39

Since Job didn't die at birth, he begins to reflect on whether he might die now. He envies the dead. No matter where they are now, it could not be as bad as sitting on an ash heap pained by sores and still grieving over his dead children.

"Why did you bring me out from the womb? Would that I had died before any eye had seen me and were as though I had not been, carried from the womb to the grave. Are not my days few? Then cease, and leave me alone, that I may find a little cheer before I go—and I shall not return—to the land of darkness and deep shadow, the land of gloom like thick darkness, like deep shadow without any order, where light is as thick darkness" (Job 10:18–22).

Now, we must admit that it would be better for some people if they had never been born; even Christ said this of Judas. In fact, the same can be said of every unbeliever.

But no believer ever has to say it would be better if they had not been born. We might feel that way, but we need not, for God's eternal purposes will become clear. What we must do is to give God time; we have all of eternity to make up for Earth's disappointments.

A friend of mine, whose wife left the marriage for another man, said he would go to bed at night hoping he wouldn't wake up in the morning. Yes, there are times when death seems better than life.

THE SIGH OF DESPAIR—
LONGING FOR GOD

Job launches into one of the greatest soliloquies ever uttered by mortal man. He contemplates what he would say if he were to talk with God. Like a friend of mine who said, "I've got a ten-page letter I'd like to leave on God's desk," Job prepares the speech he would give if God actually gave him the time of day. He vacillates between hope and despair.

On the one hand, he thinks God might just ignore him, and all attempts to speak with the Almighty are futile. God might simply use His awesome power to pulverize Job and make him of no account. He might be put out of God's sight forever.

On the other hand, Job contemplates the "hiddenness" of God, the fact that He is playing hide and seek—now you see Him, now you don't. Job is finding it hard to get through to God; we might say that the Almighty's phone is disconnected. No voicemail, no email, no way to contact God.

Let us read a few verses:

"Today also my complaint is bitter; my hand is heavy on account of my groaning. Oh, that I knew where I might find him, that I might come even to his seat! I would lay my case before him and fill my mouth with arguments." Job goes on to say, "Behold, I go forward, but he is not there, and backward, but I do not perceive him; on the left hand when he is working, I do not behold him; he turns to the right hand, but I do not see him. But he knows the way that I take; when he has tried me, I shall come out as gold" (Job 23:2–4; 8–10).

The Puritans frequently spoke of deserted souls, those Christians who lack a sense of God's favorable presence. God does this, they said, so that faith might be refined. At times, God will feel as far away from us as the farthest star. He simply hides Himself and almost seems to say, "I dare you to find Me!"

So where is God in Job's experience? Why this withdrawal, this hiding when one of His children needs Him so desperately? Eventually, we will find the answer, but for now, Job is mystified at why God cannot be found.

THE SIGH OF REGRESSION—
LONGING FOR THE GOOD OLD DAYS

Job wonders aloud why everything can't be like it once was. He longs for the days when his children were around him and God was watching over him. He remembers when he was treated with respect, when the townspeople pointed to him with hushed tones. The young people would seek him out for counsel and regard him as a model in the community. Oh for the days when he could settle down and enjoy life.

"Oh, that I were as in the months of old, as in the days when God watched over me, when his lamp shone upon my head, and by his light I walked through darkness, as I was in my prime, when the friendship of God was upon my tent, when the Almighty was yet with me, when my children were all around me" (Job 29:2–5).

Imagine what it must have meant for Job to fall from a position of power and influence. I once read a book detailing a Christian man's rise to fame in a large organization only to be brought down when a scandal made national news. He had been a pastor to pastors, a man who was revered for his integrity and leadership. But now he was implicated in a fiasco and spent sixteen months in jail. He tells about the agony and the humiliation and shame of having to say goodbye to his wife and children to return to his prison cell. If only he could have turned the clock back to the way it once was!

Someone said to the publishing magnate William Randolph Hearst, "Your paper is not as good as it once was." To which he replied, "It never was." The past always seems more glorious than the present, perhaps because we filter out our negative experiences. But even if the past were more glorious, it cannot be recalled. Wishing doesn't make things better.

THE SIGH OF BETRAYAL— LONGING FOR FAIRNESS

Fifteen times in chapter 31, Job uses the word "if." He complains about the inequities of life. If he had been an evil man, then he could have accepted his fate, believing he was getting what he deserved. There doesn't seem to be any correlation between the way he lived and the way he suffered. If someone just understood him, his pain might be lessened.

"If I have walked with falsehood and my foot has hastened to deceit; (Let me be weighed in a just balance, and let God know my integrity!) if my step has turned aside from the way and my heart has gone after my eyes, and if any spot has stuck to my hands, then let me sow, and another eat, and let what grows for me be rooted out. If my heart has been enticed toward a woman, and I have lain in wait at my neighbor's door, then let my wife grind for another, and let others bow down on her" (Job 31:5–10).

His point is clear: I don't deserve this. I have tried to do everything right, and now this! Job discovered he couldn't pray as he once did, he couldn't find peace and he certainly had no answers. Job didn't understand that his lot is that of many of God's finest children who have done no wrong to deserve their hardship. Despair is the condition of many a yielded heart.

God is on His way, but Job knows it not.

GLIMPSES OF GOD'S PURPOSES

Much is unclear regarding God's purposes, but this much we see. First, *suffering tests faith*. We can see Job's determination, "Though he slay me, I will hope in him" (Job 13:15). Then again we just read these words of hope, "When he has tried me, I shall come out as gold" (23:10). When nuggets of gold are found, the ore in which it is contained is heated to a high temperature so that the gold floats to the surface. Just so, our trials bring out our faith in its clearest expression.

Why such hardship? God wants our trust. Our faith is precious to Him.

Second, *suffering purifies faith*. Let us take the mining of gold a step further. Gold is refined in intense heat. The way they know the gold is pure is when it becomes so clear that the refiner can see his face in it. The heat has then finished its work.

Suffering forces us to deal with impurities. Suddenly we discover the difference between treasures and trash. God turns on the heat until our faith is perfected and the image of Christ can be seen in us. Job had faith before his trial began, but when God is finished refining him, he will have much more.

Third, *suffering strengthens faith*. Trials do not strengthen faith immediately; in fact, difficulties might cause us to temporarily lose our faith. But as God guides us through the trial, we emerge stronger. Once God has led us through the night, the darkness loses its power.

Christ is our best example of how to survive the sighs of a suffering soul. In Gethsemane, He said that He was "very sorrowful, even to death" (Matthew 26:38). Yet He knew that His emotional turbulence didn't separate Him from His Father. "My Father, if it be possible, let this cup pass from me," He prayed (Matthew 26:39).

The cross with its horrors was now only hours away. Throughout His lifetime, He had always referred to God as His Father, but He knew that the time was coming when He would cry out, "My God, My God, why hast thou forsaken me?" (Matthew 27:46, KJV). In those moments, Christ experienced the estrangement between a sinner and a holy God. He would become legally guilty of the most despicable sins.

His rejection secured our acceptance. He was separated from God so that we would never have to experience such alienation.

Job saw Christ only vaguely, but his questions pointed to the coming Redeemer. Over two thousand years later, Christ would come and give a more complete answer to Job's questions. Job's heart cries would be met through the life, death, and resurrection of the One about whom the New Testament speaks.

To Job's questions we now turn.

CHAPTER 5

JESUS, PLEASE ANSWER JOB

Implanted within us is the quest for meaning, the desire to make sense of the world and our place in it. Some questions, of course, are more important than others. The challenge of where I will live today is not nearly as important as the question of where I will live for eternity. The question of whether I will ever be reconciled to my friend is not as important as whether I will be reconciled to God.

Job's suffering forced him to ask ultimate questions. Stripped of his creature comforts, he was now squeezed into a corner, wondering whether he could make any sense of his fragmented world.

Job had some disadvantages.

Remember, he lived before Moses. He had never read about the miracles God had done for His people when He brought them out of Egypt. He had not heard the messages of the prophets who spoke of both the severity of God and the faithfulness of God.

Job lived before the time of Christ. He couldn't look back as we do and see the love of God poured out on the cross. He didn't know the truth of Romans 8:28, "And we know that for those who love God all things work together for good…" He didn't have this revelation to help him come to terms with his prolonged, intense, and seemingly meaningless suffering.

Many years ago, G. Campbell Morgan wrote a book titled, The Answers of Jesus to Job. He reminded us that Christ is ultimately the answer to Job's dilemma; and equally important, that Christ is Job's redeemer. Though Job didn't know it, the answers he sought would be found in the One about whom he knew virtually nothing.

Job's questions are ours, and thus we too come to Christ to make sense out of our deepest longings. We will be better able to face our disappointments because we know the deepest desires of our heart will be satisfied in Him.

Let's listen to Job's cries and Christ's answer.

THE CRY FOR A MEDIATOR

Job finds himself in distress with no answers in sight. He has tried to be respectful to his friends who have resorted to history and philosophy to find a clue to his senseless suffering. But turn wherever he will, he is none the wiser.

In frustration he poses this question, "…But how can a man be in the right before God?" (Job 9:2). He is disenchanted because God always seems to demand more than Job is able to give. Job says that even if he should wash his hands, doing all that he can to make himself pure, that in the end, he might still be cast away from God. "If I wash myself with snow and cleanse my hands with lye, yet you will plunge me into a pit, and my own clothes will abhor me" (Job 9:30–31).

Tough words, but Job is desperate. God, it appears, keeps raising the bar a notch higher. And there's no way that Job's dispute can be mediated. He and God are not peers; there is no way they can "fight it out" on a level playing field.

Job longs for a mediator. "For he is not a man, as I am, that I might answer him, that we should come to trial together. There is no arbiter between us, who might lay his hand on us both" (Job 9:32–33). He is asking, "How can I get the attention of God and argue my case so that He will listen? How can we have a meeting of the minds?" Job longs for a man who can mediate the dispute, a man who can put one hand on Job's shoulder, another on God's, and bring the warring parties together.

He understood what modern man seems to forget. We are sinners, incapable of fulfilling our side of any agreement with God. Our best efforts are always tainted with self-serving motives and spiritual incompetence. The better we know ourselves, the more we despair of meeting God on His terms.

Because the gap between God and us is unbridgeable, we are in a lose-lose situation. We long for an attorney who would plead our case and represent us before God. We want Him to feel for our needs and yet speak God's language.

Christ is the answer to Job's cry and ours. "For there is one God, and there is one mediator between God and men, the man Christ Jesus, who gave himself as a ransom for all, which is the testimony given at the proper time" (1 Timothy 2:5–6).

Christ gave Himself as a ransom; He paid the price by which sinners can be released. He became our sin-bearer and represents us to God the Father. Having saved us, He is also our advocate, "My little children, I am writing these things to you so that you may not sin. But if anyone does sin, we have an advocate with the Father, Jesus Christ the righteous" (1 John 2:1).

Only Christ can bring about the reconciliation. As both God and man, He can reconcile the two parties. We lost fellowship with God because of our sins, but Christ came to plead our case, to stand in for us. Today, we are accepted in Him, we are loved through Him, and we are heard because of Him.

Job, you have what you longed for!

A CRY FOR IMMORTALITY

Understandably, Job is preoccupied with death. Man,

says Job, is like a flower that blooms and withers; the number of his days are determined and he cannot pass beyond this allotment. A tree might be cut down and grow again from its roots, but when a man dies, he never returns. "So a man lies down and rises not again; till the heavens are no more he will not awake or be roused out of his sleep" (Job 14:12).

And yet there is a longing within us to live again. Indeed, whatever mystery might lie beyond the grave, eternity is planted within our hearts. Job pleaded that God would conceal him until His wrath passed, hopeful for some contact with God in the afterlife. Though the curtain that leads beyond death was closed, Job longed for a glimmer, some shaft of light that would illumine the grave.

He then expresses his heart-cry. "If a man dies, shall he live again? All the days of my service I would wait, till my renewal should come" (v. 14). Please note that the word *again* is not in the original Hebrew manuscripts. Job is really asking, "If a man dies, will he live?" To put it another way: Does man live beyond the grave? Does his soul have a continued existence? It is not a question of resurrection, but a question of continuity.

Christ provides a more profound answer than Job could ever have realized. Not only does man's soul continue after death, but his body shall be raised. There is not only the continued existence of the soul, but the continued existence of the body.

To Martha and Mary grieving over their dead brother, Christ promised that Lazarus would rise again and then affirmed, "I am the resurrection and the life. Whoever believes in me, though he die, yet shall he live, and everyone who lives and believes in me shall never die. Do you believe this?" (John 11:25–26). Yes, those who believe in Christ shall live even if they die; in fact, they shall never really die at all!

We can take heart. Eternity can give meaning to time. God has forever to help us make sense of our trials and sorrows. This is the answer to the unfinished tasks we will lose at death; this is the answer to the deeper longings of life. A reunion at a future date is possible.

There is a story about a young woman who was trying to swim the English Channel. She became weary and called for help, asking that she be taken up into the boat that accompanied her. Once in the boat, she could see the shore; it was not as far away as she had imagined it to be. She regretted having quit and said, "If only I had seen the shore, I could have made it all the way."

Paul said, "For I consider that the sufferings of this present time are not worth comparing with the glory that is to be revealed to us" (Romans 8:18). When we lose heart, we just have to look at the shore.

Take heart if you have received more than your share of heartache. Do not let injustice injure your spirit and confidence. Look beyond this life to the harbor. Let the unanswered questions of this life increase your hope in the life to come.

A CRY FOR GOD

All of our longings can be summarized in an intense desire to see God. In fact, our greatest need is always to see Him, for then we would be satisfied. To behold the Lord is the greatest aspiration of the heart.

Here is Job's cry, "For I know that my Redeemer lives, and at the last he will stand upon the earth. And after my skin has been thus destroyed, yet in my flesh I shall see God, whom I shall see for myself, and my eyes shall behold, and not another. My heart faints within me!" (Job 19:25–27). The word used here for *Redeemer* is "Goel," a qualified "next of kin" who can redeem us. This is a cry for an avenger who would stand with Job in his trials.

And yet from his flesh he "would see God." This has been interpreted in two ways. Job might have meant "*without* my flesh I shall see God," that is, he will see God even if his body is in the grave. Or perhaps he did mean "*in* his flesh he would see God," that is, in a resurrected body. This would be consistent with his conviction that he would see God with his own eyes. The central point is that he was conscious of the continuation of his personality.

Thousands of years later, Christ appeared on the banks

of the Jordan river as the "Lamb of God, who takes away the sin of the world" (John 1:29). Job was saved on credit. God anticipated that his sins would be laid on the coming Redeemer, and thus Job had fellowship with God long before Christ came to Earth. Job was saved by the work of Christ just as surely as the apostle Paul, Martin Luther, or Billy Graham.

Yes, even Job was saved because of Christ, the Redeemer. And thanks to Christ, Job has already had his wish fulfilled. The saints of the Old Testament have, I believe, already arrived within the portals of heaven. Job is among them. This stricken man realized that someday he would see God, *and he has.*

Again, Christ is the fulfillment of Job's cry. Not only is He Job's redeemer, but He affirmed, "Whoever has seen me has seen the Father" (John 14:9). Thus, the disciples saw God in the flesh. We will someday get to see Christ, too, and we shall even behold the Father face to face.

MORE LESSONS FROM JOB'S CRIES

Job expressed the deepest aspirations of the human heart. His cries remind us that *difficult questions lead us to ultimate questions.* Job began by trying to unravel the question of his own suffering. He ends up by asking about eternity. The disappointments in this life forced him to anticipate possible blessings in the life to come. He began by being obsessed with his immediate need, but ended by being obsessed with his quest for God.

This explains why God brings suffering into our lives. The problems of Earth make us grapple with the reality of heaven. We can only find meaning today if we look at tomorrow.

Second, our ultimate questions are not solved by finding out *what*, but *whom*. Job, of course, saw only the shadow of God's purposes; he longed for a redeemer but didn't know when one would come. For us, Christ is the focal point of our questions, the hub for the individual spokes of our existence.

Our longing for a mediator, immortality, and God Himself become a reality in Christ the Lord, the King. And if we have seen God, we are satisfied. "No one has ever seen God; the only God, who is at the Father's side, he has made him known" (John 1:18). The unknown God becomes knowable in Christ; He has introduced us to the Father.

God has suffered along with us. There on the cross we see He has not stayed afar off, but is near.

Come with me to a concentration camp. The women have been beaten, abused, and humiliated. Corrie Ten Boom was having a Bible study in the camp when a woman angrily shouted "Is this what your God has done?" The bitter woman takes the bandages from her hands and shows her broken fingers, now gnarled and pained. "I played first violin in a symphony...and now look at this...is this what your God has done?"

Silence.

Corrie Ten Boom answers quietly, "All that we know is that Jesus Christ, God Himself, suffered for us that we might be lovingly reconciled to Him."

At times, that is about all we know in answer to such questions. The Redeemer has stood upon the Earth. And with resurrected eyes, we shall see Him as He is.

Augustine prayed, "No man hath seen God and lived...O God, let me die that I might see Thee and be satisfied."

Our greatest need is always to see God. The longing of every soul can be fulfilled, not with answers, but by the person of God. And knowing Him, the answers themselves become less important.

CHAPTER 6

WORDS OF WISDOM FROM A YOUNG MAN

The greatest stumbling block Christianity faces is the problem of evil. We've all been asked, "Where was your God during the Holocaust?" If God is all powerful and good, why doesn't He remove the evil from Earth?

There are two possible ways we can escape the dilemma. First, we can simply deny that God is omnipotent. That was the position of William James who believed that God would do away with evil if He could, but He can't; we should be thankful, James taught, because He's doing the best He can.

A second solution is to simply affirm that God is not good in any understandable sense. If God is indifferent to human suffering, then so be it. Of course, neither of these two solutions is acceptable. The Bible affirms both the power of God and the love of God.

If the problem of evil is baffling to us who believe the Bible, think of the stumbling block it is to the unconverted.

The book of Job confronts this problem only through a narrow lens; it does so through the life and struggles of one righteous man. The question is not so much why there is evil in the world, but why a righteous man should experience so much of it.

Job felt the full weight of this dilemma. He had served God faithfully and was rewarded with ten dead children and painful boils. And to make matters worse, he had three friends who blamed him for his calamity. In effect, they told him, "Job, if you weren't wicked, this wouldn't have happened to you."

Listening to this monotonous dialogue was a young man named Elihu who was itching to speak. The moment there was a lull in the conversation, he spoke up. In fact, he took Zophar's turn to speak a third time.

First, Elihu was angry. Angry at Job because, "he justified himself rather than God" (Job 32:2). Under criticism, Job had retreated into self-justification. Like most of us, when false accusations come our way, we are tempted to rummage through our lives and pull out every scrap of good we have ever done. The more Job's friends condemned him, the more he defended himself. He began to sound nauseatingly self-righteous. He ends up saying that God was unjust because He was punishing a righteous man.

Unlike Job's friends, Elihu didn't accuse Job of sinful works, but he did accuse him of self-righteous words. In fact, he actually quotes Job's words back to him. He limits himself to what he has heard from Job's mouth, not hearsay.

Elihu will give a different interpretation of Job's suffering. Neither Job's self-justification nor the condemnation of his friends was correct. Elihu will point Job to God, affirming His right to do what He wishes with His servant.

Elihu was angry with Job's friends "because they had found no answer, although they had declared Job to be in the wrong" (32:3). These men believed that all suffering was punishment for sin; so according to their premises, Job had greatly sinned. Not all that the friends said was wrong, but their accusations were distorted.

Second, though Elihu was angry, he spoke hesitantly. He was young and didn't know if he should answer. But young people cannot tolerate hypocrisy. They are the first to know whether we are telling the whole truth.

Elihu felt constrained to speak. He says, "For I am full of words; the spirit within me constrains me. Behold, my belly is like wine that has no vent; like new wineskins ready to burst. I must speak, that I may find relief; I must open my lips and answer" (32:18–20). It was as if he had his thumb on a garden hose; the pressure of the moment took over. A torrent of words came out of his mouth.

Who is Elihu? An impertinent young man or a wise young theologian? Some have described him as a conceited young man who stumbles into the conversation and thinks he's called of God to set everyone else straight. But unlike Job's other three friends, Elihu is not rebuked at the end of the book.

Others have spoken so highly of him that they think he was a pre-incarnate revelation of Jesus Christ. This is unlikely because he admits he is but a man. He makes no claims that would lead us to think he was deity, but he speaks much that is right and good.

Though we have few clues about him personally, judging by what he said, we have to describe him as brilliant and provocative. Of course, he doesn't have the vantage point of the New Testament, so his perspective is limited. But given his times and circumstances, his remarks are insightful. This is the one speech in the book to which Job does not reply. Perhaps it left him speechless.

Elihu forms an important transition in the book. He prepares us for God's personal revelation that is soon to come.

GOD IS SOVEREIGN

Elihu begins by saying that God is sovereign; He is not like a man who must give account. Then he quotes Job's words back to him and adds his commentary. "I am pure, without transgression; I am clean, and there is no iniquity in me" (Job 33:9). But Elihu asks, "Why do you contend against him, saying, 'He will answer none of man's words'?

For God speaks in one way, and in two, though man does not perceive it" (33:13–14).

Yes, self-righteous remarks did come from Job's lips. Job, Elihu contended, was accusing God of dealing unfairly with an innocent man. But Job was not completely innocent. Job thought God was obligated to treat him with blessings because of his righteous life, but God is under no obligation to do so. God is God and man is man. If we are blessed, it's because of God's mercy, not because we deserve it.

There is little use trying to get God to reveal His secrets. He doesn't allow us to read His diary; He doesn't let us read the fine print in His plans. Indeed, Elihu says that God has every right to plead the Fifth Amendment! "When he is quiet, who can condemn? When he hides his face, who can behold him, whether it be a nation or a man?" (34:29). Let's not try to force His hand—it will lead to futility.

Yes, God is not only greater than man, He is also different from man. He plays by an entirely different set of rules. Elihu didn't use this example, but we know that God doesn't live by the commandment, "Thou shalt not steal." Simply put, the commandment doesn't apply to God because He owns everything! He can give to Job and take from him because He owns it all.

Why should Job strive with God? Elihu affirms that God is greater than man and does not reveal His secrets. Samuel Ridout, in his commentary on Job wrote, "Let the potsherds of the earth strive with one another; God will not stoop to such a conflict." God is too exalted to enter into controversy with us. We shouldn't expect Him to bow to our desire for explanations or special blessings.

As long as we raise questions about the character of God, we are in no position to have our questions answered. God is limited only by His own nature and the plans He chooses. Because humans need accountability, we assume God does too. There is no one to whom He reports; He does not have a yearly review or run His plans past a committee.

Is this frightening? It might be if God could not be trusted, but thankfully, He can be.

GOD IS TRUSTWORTHY

Elihu tells us that God can be believed. Job had said that it didn't pay to serve God because the Almighty was so unpredictable. Well, yes, His ways are beyond us, but this should not lead us to despair, for God is good and just. "Therefore, hear me, you men of understanding: far be it from God that he should do wickedness, and from the Almighty that he should do wrong. For according to the work of a man he will repay him, and according to his ways he will make it befall him. Of a truth, God will not do wickedly, and the Almighty will not pervert justice" (Job 34:10–12).

"Far be it from God that he should do wickedness."

That is true by definition, for evil (wickedness) is that which comes short of the glory of God. There is no independent standard in the universe by which He can be judged. He is His own measure and abides by the laws He voluntarily imposes on Himself; we are to abide by the laws He imposes on us. Thankfully, He cannot lie because He cannot deny Himself.

We can be encouraged because He always acts according to justice and He has all the facts. He knows the end from the beginning. When men are judged, it will not be with distorted or partial information.

One day when my daughter came home from college, she brought a notebook full of questions. She pulled up a chair and asked her first question. "What if God wanted to be alone again?" Elihu asks a similar question: What would happen if God were to turn toward Himself and no longer support His creation? One result would be that "all flesh would perish together, and man would return to dust" (34:15).

God can, however, be trusted to keep His promises to us. And these promises are as eternal as He Himself is.

Remember that Elihu was angry both with Job who justified himself, and with his three friends who condemned him. What they overlooked was that God could use tragedy not just to punish but also to refine. He calls God a teacher and His purpose is to take those who are righteous and lead them to increased faith. "Behold, God is exalted in his power; who is a teacher like him?" (36:22).

Although Job also saw this, Elihu makes an important contribution to the dialogue. Sometimes discipline is punishment for sin; sometimes it's simply God's way of deepening our relationship with Him.

Either way, God can be trusted to do what is in line with our own ultimate good. Job had found fault with God because God's judgment was not in accordance with Job's short-sighted expectations. As long as Job accuses God, he gets no answer; when he submits, he receives comfort even without explanations.

Suffering forces us to confront God. Our struggles give us little choice except to probe the depths of the Almighty. The outcome should be greater faith, less human wisdom, and more confidence in God. Either we will be driven closer to God or we will turn against Him. Suffering never leaves us where it found us.

GOD IS HIDDEN

Elihu appears comfortable with a God who hides Himself from men. Though He speaks to us, we cannot see Him. We know that He is there, but we cannot fathom His ways. Lightning and thunder remind us of His power, but they give us little insight into God's thoughts toward us. The sunshine reminds us of His love and earthquakes are a picture of His judgment. Such mixed messages are confusing and do not reassure us of God's personal concern. In this life, the rain falls on the just and the unjust. The same can be said for tornadoes and tidal waves.

A girl who walked under the stars said to her mother, "Heaven even looks beautiful from the wrong side." So it is. The starry heavens remind us of the power of God, but they do not tell us everything we want to know. Nature leaves us unsatisfied. To quote Elihu, "God thunders wondrously with his voice; he does great things that we cannot comprehend" (Job 37:5).

We also know that God speaks to us in suffering. But that too is subject to various interpretations. C.S. Lewis was right when he said that God speaks to us in our joys but "shouts to us in our pain." But even then, we often don't know what He is saying.

Elihu appropriately ends his speech by saying, "The Almighty—we cannot find him; he is great in power; justice and abundant righteousness he will not violate. Therefore men fear him; he does not regard any who are wise in their own conceit" (37:23–24). Job would be better served if he were to just worship God without trying to figure Him out.

God reveals Himself to man and thus gives us glimpses of His ways. But for the most part, He remains hidden, giving us just enough of Himself to make us long for more.

THE GOD WHO HIDES AND SEEKS

The fact that God is hidden does not mean that He is merely the figment of our imagination. Some people have argued that the mystery of God demonstrates the indifference or even absence of God. Not so. Indeed, the fact of God is as certain as the fact of the sun.

Years ago, I taught apologetics—that is, the defense of the Christian faith. We would spend several hours analyzing the arguments for God's existence, trying to evaluate them logically. I seldom do that anymore for one reason—I've concluded that to give arguments for God's existence is like lighting a candle to see if one can find the sun!

The atheist cannot explain the existence of the mind he uses to think his atheistic thoughts. He is like a tree affirming that it has no roots or like a fish in the ocean denying the existence of water. Yes, God is hidden, but that should not be interpreted to mean that He does not exist.

Second, *the "hiddenness" of God does not mean the disinterestedness of God.* In other words, God is always directly and continually involved in His creation. Elihu puts it this way, "For his eyes are on the ways of a man, and he sees all his steps" (Job 34:21). The silence of God should not be interpreted as the indifference of God.

All of us have experienced "divine appointments" in our life—those times when we have seen God's providence even in little things. Indeed, a sparrow cannot fall without the Father's notice. It may stretch our faith to believe that God loves us, but that's what we are required to believe if we want to be Christians. It is precisely such faith that honors God.

Finally, *the "hiddenness" of God does not mean that God has not revealed Himself at all.* Indeed, even here in the book of Job, God will come on the scene and speak to Job directly. He doesn't play games with us, though sometimes we see Him, and sometimes we don't.

Even that revelation, however, is vague in comparison to God's revelation to us in Christ. We read, "For the law was given through Moses; grace and truth came through Jesus Christ. No one has ever seen God; the only God, who is at the Father's side, he has made him known" (John 1:17–18). Christ affirmed, "Whoever has seen me has seen the Father" (John 14:9).

Yes, grace and truth came by Jesus Christ. Yet even in Christ, we only see as much of God as we can take, namely only a part of His character, plans, and purposes. Even Paul, who knew God better than the rest of us, wrote, "We see in a mirror dimly" (1 Corinthians 13:12). Thankfully, we do see, but there is still much mystery.

All of this should motivate us to probe the depths of God, to know Him as far as He can become known in this life. And no matter how much there is to know, every mountain we climb will lead to another one. "Can you find out the deep things of God? Can you find out the limit of the Almighty?" (Job 11:7) Answer that for yourself!

Enough said. Job will not confront the God he thought he knew. But his concept of the Almighty will be radically revised. Let us be silent and listen.

CHAPTER 7

WHEN GOD COMES

Have you ever had a conversation that wearied you? The repetition was nauseating. The old ideas didn't improve with their retelling. You are no wiser than when it all began. You hear the words but you have stopped listening.

I heard about an old woman who lost her hearing. When asked whether she wanted to have a hearing aid, she replied, "No, I'm one hundred years old and I've heard it all!"

Job would understand. He is tired of hearing speeches, tired of listening to the voice of a man. He wants to hear from God Himself. In his closing speech, he says, "Let the Almighty answer me!" (Job 31:35). Who of us hasn't wished that God would show up and talk to us directly, giving the final verdict on whatever troubles us?

Job got his wish.

Out of the whirlwind came the voice of God! This was the same voice that Adam and Eve heard in the Garden of Eden; this was the voice that told Moses to remove his shoes from his feet. This was the voice that thundered at Sinai.

Although I am not so presumptuous as to think that God needs an introduction, there are several observations we should make before we ponder His words to Job.

First, *God allowed time to pass before He spoke.* He waited for human speculation to be totally exhausted. Some scholars believe that two years had passed since Job's trial began. Of course, we should not be surprised God waited so long; it's remarkable that He responded at all. Sometimes He has been silent for centuries!

Second, we should not be surprised to discover that *He disregarded all that was said.* He doesn't begin by saying, "Now I know you have had a long talk; some things said were good, others were just plain wrong." He doesn't make so much as one direct reference to the speeches that have preceded His. Nor does He say, "Job, you really have been hurting, and I'm glad I can take you out of your misery. In fact, I want to tell you why you suffered!"

God ignores Job's friends and speaks directly to Job himself. When the Almighty asks, "Who is this that darkens counsel by words without knowledge?" (Job 38:2), God isn't referring to Elihu but to Job. Job has spoken words without knowledge; the light of truth was lost in a smoke cloud of unbelief and self-pity.

Finally, *God speaks out of the whirlwind.* This dramatic intervention must have caught Job by surprise. We don't know whether he saw a representation of God or just heard a voice. What we do know is that once the words were heard, Job knew this was not the voice of a man, but of God.

So, what does God have to say? He will have an answer to Job's suffering, but it's not the answer we expect. When the encounter is over, we are going to be both satisfied and dissatisfied; our knowledge will be greatly increased, but we will leave wishing we knew more.

God begins by asking Job a series of rhetorical questions. One question follows another in rapid succession. God knows that Job doesn't know the answers, so He doesn't even wait for a reply. God just wants Job to get the point, a point we will come to at the end of the chapter.

LISTENING TO GOD SPEAK

God's questions will help Job to see his problems in perspective.

First, God proves that He—not Job—has authority over the realm of nature. "Where were you when I laid the foundation of the earth? Tell me, if you have understanding. Who determined its measurements—surely you know! Or who stretched the line upon it? On what were its bases sunk, or who laid its cornerstone? (Job 38:4–6).

Job didn't understand nature as we do today. He didn't know that every snowflake was different; he had no idea as to how hail was formed. Yet the Lord asks him, "Have you entered the storehouses of the snow, or have you seen the storehouses of the hail?" (v. 22). Not even a scientist today could answer such questions.

God now asks Job about the stars, the constellations, the ordinances of the heavens and their "rule on the earth" (v. 33). Job didn't know that the observable universe was actually more than 90 billion light years in diameter and that it was populated with trillions upon trillions of stars. He might have known more than we give him credit for, but when God was finished, *Job knew how little he knew.*

The point? God is helping Job come to the humbling realization that he doesn't know much about the whys and wherefores of nature and God's work of sustaining the universe. And if he can't understand these matters, he most assuredly is not capable of commenting on God's moral government.

To Job's credit, though he knew little about the starry heavens, he worshipped. Today's scientists know much more but are willing to regard creation as a random fluke in an impersonal universe. Sadly, evolutionists disregard all natural reason and actually believe that nothing times nobody equals everything! To think that the universe came about by chance is equivalent to believing there was an explosion in a print factory and the result was Webster's Dictionary!

God continues to remind Job that He is the Lord of animate nature, the living plants and animals. God created the universe that it might be inhabited. The beasts of prey, the wild goats, the horses, hawks, and eagles were all created by God. "Is it by your understanding that the hawk soars and spreads his wings toward the south? Is it at your command that the eagle mounts up and makes his nest on high?" (Job 39:26–27).

Consider the migration of birds. The ability they have to fly from Alaska to the southern islands with a trajectory so accurate that if their angle of flight were off by one degree they would miss their landing point. Even when they are blown off course by a storm, they regain their sense of direction above the unmarked ocean. Scientists are still trying to understand their navigational systems.

Humanistic scientists should sit with Job, listening to the voice of God. Modern science can talk learnedly of the solar system, the laws of gravitation, and can explain the rotation of heavenly bodies, but who has established these laws? How did the solar system originate? Who regulates the complex conditions needed for that delicate process we call life?

To paraphrase Socrates, "What is human knowledge but knowledge of our ignorance?" David wrote, "O LORD, how manifold are your works! In wisdom have you made them all; the earth is full of your creatures" (Psalm 104:24).

God challenges Job to find fault with Him. "Shall a faultfinder contend with the Almighty? He who argues with God, let him answer it" (Job 40:2). If Job could not answer one of God's questions about the physical realm, why does he dare intrude into the metaphysical realm—that is, the realm beyond nature where God's agenda is even more enigmatic and obscure to mortals?

JOB'S RESPONSE

Job admits he has talked too much. His speeches were too long, his comments impertinent. He cries, "Behold, I am of small account; what shall I answer you? I lay my hand on my mouth. I have spoken once, and I will not answer; twice, but I will proceed no further" (Job 40:4–5). This is the man who earlier had said he would like to talk to God directly; he would like to take God to court and bring lengthy arguments against Him. Now that Job has the chance to speak, he's reduced to silence in the presence of a God who knows infinitely more than he.

God still isn't finished. He gives further proof that He has exclusive rights to the moral and spiritual realm. God hammers His point home by giving Job the opportunity to play God. "Will you even put me in the wrong? Will you condemn me that you may be in the right? Have you an arm like God, and can you thunder with a voice like his? Adorn yourself with majesty and dignity; clothe yourself with glory and splendor....Look on everyone who is proud and bring him low... Then will I also acknowledge to you that your own right hand can save you" (Job 40:8–10; 12; 14).

Job, can you do what I do? Can you thunder like I do? Can you take proud people and make them humble? Can the acts that are ascribed to Me be ascribed to you? Are you really going to set Me straight? Prove that I acted arbitrarily! Tell Me what I'm doing wrong!

Here is the situation as it stands. In effect, God is saying to Job, "Either you are right and I'm wrong, or else you are wrong and I'm right. Which do you think it is?"

Job now has a new standard of measurement. In his speeches, he was always comparing himself with others; he thought he was better than they. His friends compared themselves with Job and thought they were better than he. Now in the presence of God, none of this matters. The long speeches are trivial and wholly irrelevant.

Job says, "I know that you can do all things, and that no purpose of yours can be thwarted....Therefore I have uttered what I did not understand, things too wonderful for me, which I did not know....I had heard of you by the hearing of the ear, but now my eye sees you; therefore I despise myself, and repent in dust and ashes" (Job 42:2–3, 5–6).

God runs the world as He wishes. If He wants to bring

trials into one person's life but not another, He has that right. To some He brings prosperity, to others poverty. Some enjoy good health, others live with constant pain. This is the way God has chosen to run His world.

JOB'S TWO ERRORS

Job was wrong. Very wrong.

First, *he underestimated God.* God was *bigger* than he realized. Job can observe the stars, but it was God who created them. God not only understands the elaborate laws of nature, but He set them up. This is the God from whom nothing is hidden.

God was not only bigger than Job realized, God was also *better* than he realized. This was a God who created animals and plants only after He had created a home for them; this was the God who had a well-calculated plan for everything. The smallest detail was not run according to whim, but according to wisdom. The universe was not random, but divinely ordered.

God was also *purer* than Job realized. There in the presence of God, Job was not only aware of his own ignorance, but also his own sinfulness. Job repents, not just because of the limitations of his mind, but also because of the iniquity of his heart.

He thought that God was much like he was. He thought he could figure God out; but God was bigger and better than he ever dreamed.

When a mother was grieving at the death of her son, her pastor wisely told her, "God is too good to do anything evil and too wise to make a mistake!" God is bigger, better, and wiser than we are. He is also infinitely pure and holy. Our temptation is to underestimate Him!

Second, *Job overestimated himself.* Of course, this is really the opposite side of the coin—when we underestimate God, we always overestimate ourselves. Job admitted, "Therefore I have uttered what I did not understand, things too wonderful for me, which I did not know" (Job 42:3). By judging God, he was venturing into territory about which he was ignorant. Worship God, yes; judge Him, no. Alexander Pope recognized our tendency to judge God and question His motives. In *An Essay On Man*, Pope rebukes man for this by saying we "Snatch from his hand the Balance and the Rod, Re-judge his Justice, Be the GOD of GOD!"

No wonder we are frustrated! On the one hand, we are created with eternity in our hearts, so we ask many great questions; on the other, we do not have enough information to answer these questions. To put it differently, we seek the answers to ultimate questions, but we are limited by space, time, and knowledge. We are driven to search for answers that we cannot find.

Job overestimated his knowledge of God. He thought

God should act in predictable ways; he thought God should reward the righteous and punish the guilty so that the distinction between the two would be clear to a watching world. He thought God owed him an explanation if there were exceptions to this rule.

There is a story about a museum guide who would direct his tour group to look up at a haphazard mass of tangled strings of all colors and sizes. To them it appeared as if they were seeing something that might have been made by the random effort of school children.

Then the guide took the tourists up the stairs where they could see the top of this display. They found themselves admiring a beautiful tapestry, a giant rug that caught the attention of every eye.

Look at life and you will often see nothing but the random jumble of unrelated events. We are looking at God's plan from below. In some future day when we look at it from above, we will see the wisdom in it all. For now we don't have to see the tapestry, we just have to trust the Weaver.

I once heard of a Christian couple whose four-month-old baby died from sudden infant death syndrome. There is little use trying to speculate what God's hidden purpose might be in this. We are left with the dangling threads; we do not see the tapestry.

Only faith can bridge the gap between God's greatness

and our finiteness. God did not give Job the answer he expected, but the Almighty did give him an answer: *trust Me*. Job is to grow in his confidence in God's wisdom and goodness. Job is to trust God in all of those areas where he can only *probe* but never *prove*.

To put it clearly: It is not necessary for us to know the hidden purposes of God, it is only necessary to know the revealed person of God. As the song goes, when we cannot trace His hand, we must simply trust His heart.

We have to agree with Job who, in effect, said, "I was talking when I should have been listening; I was whining when I should have been worshipping. I thought I could reason with God, but 'His ways [are] past finding out'" (Romans 11:33, KJV). Speculation is not wrong, it's just inaccurate.

When I was a boy, I would walk behind my father who was carrying the lantern in the darkness of night. That old lantern gave only enough light to see the path; it didn't give enough light to show us where the path was leading. And yet, I was not concerned about where the path might lead as long as my father knew. We only had to walk one step at a time.

We are not told where the path will lead; we are only told that we should trust the Guide. And the better we know Him, the more we can trust Him. Anxiety comes when we bear burdens for those things which are out of our control. But that which is out of our control is firmly in God's hands.

How long can you put up with a difficult journey? That depends on how well you know the guide. If you know him well, you will endure anything. You will have confidence that there must be a purpose.

The better you and I know God, the less He has to tell us about His ways. By nature, we either want to look behind us to see what God has done, or we want to look ahead to find out what lies around the bend. God asks only that we stay close to Him.

Our advantage is that we know God through the revelation of Jesus Christ. A woman angrily asked a pastor, "Where was your God when my son was killed?" to which he replied, "He was in the same place He was when His Son was killed." We know He has become involved in our predicament and has extended His grace to us.

Our challenge is to believe.

CHAPTER 8

THE PURPOSE OF IT ALL

On November 8, 1994, Pastor Duane Scott Willis, his wife, and six of their eight children were driving on I-94 en route to Milwaukee when they hit a metal brace that had fallen from a semi a few hundred feet ahead of them. Scott knew he couldn't miss hitting the object, so he chose to run over it directly, hoping it would do less damage than if he hit it with his tires.

The metal punctured the gas tank, and by the time the van was brought to a standstill, it was already in flames. Five of their six children died instantly in the inferno; a sixth child, Ben, died a few hours later. The pastor and his wife, Janet, escaped with first and second degree burns.

"God has been preparing us for this moment," Scott said to Janet as the flames shot into the air. The story of courage and faith was beamed throughout the nation by radio and television. People were surprised by the steady confidence of this couple whose faith in God was not shaken in the face of a massive personal tragedy. Even cynics admitted that for some people, faith in God is real—*undeniably* real in confronting unexpected loss.

Can we see a purpose in such a tragedy? Yes, Scott and Janet have been a witness to a skeptical world. Whenever they appeared on television, they spoke about the comfort that God gave them; they spoke openly of their knowledge that they had not permanently lost their children. At least some rationale for this tragedy can be discerned in this life.

In the book of Job we have a similar scenario. Job's children were killed in a windstorm, his wealth was destroyed, his health was gone, and there appeared to be no purpose in it all. But there was a happy ending. Job was now blessed more than he had ever been blessed before.

When the sun shines again, when a ministry or marriage is restored, when God is glorified by the faith of His people, such positive results help us make sense out of it all. Most often, however, God's people do not experience such a storybook ending. For every tragedy where we can discern some rationale, there is another one that appears senseless and without redeeming value.

As we have learned, we are often frustrated because we cannot find meaning in the ambiguities of life. Since we cannot see God's hidden purpose, we are given to speculation. We long to see a pattern even when there is none; we want to see the flower that our tears have watered.

The book of Job teaches us that there is meaning in our suffering, but it might not be the purpose we think it is. We must believe that there is a purpose even in those trials where we cannot see beneficial results.

Job was fortunate in that his story ended with direct benefits that came as a result of the trial.

JOB'S NEW CONCEPT OF GOD

In the last chapter, we noticed that Job had underestimated God and overestimated himself. Now he admits, "I know that you can do all things, and that no purpose of yours can be thwarted" (Job 42:2). He understands that God is not accountable to anyone. Job had wanted to question God, but when invited to do so, he falls silent.

Job also understands that God is unpredictable. We cannot judge a man's spiritual life by the number of trials he endures. God sometimes acts outside the boundaries of our own comfort zones. This unpredictability is frightening because we would like the future to proceed along predictable lines. But it's also comforting: God often acts more graciously toward us than we could ever dream. Though He cannot be depended upon to do as we think He should, He can be depended upon to walk with us through what He gives us. And if we know Him, He can be depended upon to do what is best for us.

God commends Job for speaking of Him that "which was right." Job spoke rightly about God, not when he bitterly complained about his plight, nor even during those special flashes of confidence that surfaced in his grief. No, Job spoke most correctly when he praised God's greatness and affirmed that, "No purpose of yours can be thwarted" (Job 42:2).

Job grew in his understanding and appreciation of God, but this didn't lessen the mystery that surrounds the Almighty. Getting closer to God doesn't dissipate the perplexity; indeed, knowing God better only increases it! Those who don't know God may think they have Him pretty well figured out. Men such as Moses and Job who actually met Him would say that God's ways are assuredly "past finding out" (Job 9:10, KJV). The better we know Him, the more certain we are that we know very little.

JOB'S NEW MINISTRY FOR GOD

God spoke to Eliphaz as the leader of the trio of counselors saying, "My anger burns against you and against your two friends, for you have not spoken of me what is right, as my servant Job has" (Job 42:7). Then the Almighty added, "Now therefore take seven bulls and seven rams and go to my servant Job and offer up a burnt offering for yourselves. And my servant Job shall pray for you, for I will accept his prayer not to deal with you according to your folly. For you have not spoken of me what is right, as my servant Job has" (42:8).

Job's prayers averted God's judgment on these friends who spoke about God and His ways. God accepted Job's sacrifice and prayers on their behalf.

Wherein did Job's friends err? They certainly maintained God's righteousness. They had denounced evil; they thought they had vindicated God by blaming Job for the evil that had come upon him. Despite what might have been the best of intentions, they had a wrong view of God and thus of themselves. For what we think about God determines what we think about everything else.

They thought our relationship with God was based on works, not grace. They thought they had escaped trials because they were better than Job; they did not realize that the reason was because God was being kinder to them than they deserved. Their warped understanding of God gave them permission to self-righteously exalt themselves.

Years ago, a book was written titled, *Why Bad Things Happen To Good People.* Perhaps one should be written titled, *Why Good Things Happen To Bad People.* The latter surely is just as great a mystery as the former. The reason Job's friends were so well off is not because they were righteous, but because God is generous.

They did not understand grace.

God was displeased with the idea that suffering is

always a direct consequence of personal sin and failure. He was angry when they pinned everything on Job saying that if he were honest, he would admit to the sin that caused his calamity. Sure, Job was a sinner; yes, he had even sinned by speaking self-righteously, but haven't we all done the same? God Himself had said of Job, "There is none like him on the earth, a blameless and upright man, who fears God and turns away from evil" (Job 1:8).

Incredibly, their roles and that of Job are reversed! While rendering those dreary speeches, not once did his three friends think for a moment that *they* might have been the object of God's anger. As it turns out, they do not instruct Job about God, Job now instructs them! Unless they are willing to be prayed for by the very person whom they regarded with contempt, they will be judged by God. Job acted as a priest, and they were restored to God and to their friend.

Interestingly, we read, "And the LORD restored the fortunes of Job, when he had prayed for his friends. And the LORD gave Job twice as much as he had before" (42:10). Job had to be reconciled to his friends, forgiving them for their harsh words before he received blessing from God.

Job's new ministry even extends to us. James writes, "Behold, we consider those blessed who remained steadfast. You have heard of the steadfastness of Job, and you have seen the purpose of the Lord, how the Lord is compassionate and merciful" (James 5:11). He did not know that for four thousand years, millions of people would be encouraged and instructed through his life and example. He did not know that his distress would be an object lesson that would bring glory to God.

JOB'S NEW PROSPERITY FROM GOD

There is an Old Testament law which says a person must restore double that which was lost or stolen. God didn't steal these things from Job; indeed, God cannot steal for He owns everything. He was under no obligation to restore Job's fortunes, but He does. This was yet another display of the unpredictable mercy of God. Job went from having seven thousand sheep to fourteen thousand; the three thousand camels were now six thousand; and the five hundred yoke of oxen and five hundred female donkeys became one thousand of each.

Let's count his children, "He had also seven sons and three daughters." Now, that is exactly the number Job had in chapter one. We might be tempted to think that his children didn't double in number. But think about it: The children who died in the storm were not lost, they were only relocated. They were in heaven and once Job and the other children joined them, he would have fourteen sons and six daughters!

Job's wife, I'm sure, was grateful that God gave her

more children in this life. Interestingly, even though she had encouraged her husband to curse God and die, she is not rebuked here. Her remark was borne of desperation and loving concern.

Consider Job's longevity. He lived 140 years after his trial. This has led to speculation that he might have been 70 when the trial came and therefore, God doubled the length of his life. If so, he would have lived twice as long after his trial as he did before. He would have died at age 210.

What can we say in summary of this awesome book?

First, *God is worthy of worship even when worship doesn't appear profitable.* Satan tried to make the point that God has to dangle rewards in front of a man to entice him to spiritual obedience and service. Recall that he said that Job served God simply because the Almighty had made a hedge about him and "blessed the work of his hands" (Job 1:10).

Would God have been worthy of worship even if God had not restored the fortunes of Job and given him double of everything? Would God have been worthy of worship even if Job had died in chapter 32 rather than chapter 42? Do we have a right to see the rewards of worship in this life?

No, we do not. God was worthy of worship long before Job was doubly blessed. Many righteous, obedient people have died in prisons, concentration camps, and plane crashes. They will have to wait for heaven to see the good that came from their obedience.

Second, *we learn that God and the devil are both involved in our tests.* Notice that it says here that Job's friends came and "comforted him for all the evil that the LORD had brought upon him" (Job 42:11). The trial came from God even though it was brought to Job through the work of Satan.

Let's consider the experience of the Willis family. How should they interpret the tragic accident back in 1994? Was this truly an accident? Or is "accident" just our word for an inexplicable occurrence?

Think of it: They were traveling to visit their son in Wisconsin because their church was being used as a polling place that particular election day. They could have started out a minute later or a minute earlier. Or the truck could have been a few hundred yards ahead or behind them. The piece of metal could have been a foot or two to the left or to the right and the gas tank would not have been punctured. Humanly speaking, the crash was a fluke.

But for the Willis family, this was not fate; it was the meticulous planning of Providence. They can say with confidence, "It is God who took our six children to Himself."

What we call an accident is an event planned by God for purposes which may or may not be known to us. What we call an "if only" is really a "divine appointment." Blessed are those who see God in the heartaches of life.

Third, *all trials have one revealed purpose: to trust God even without further explanations.* We must believe that He knows what He's doing even when it seems contrary to our best interests. This, we can be sure, is the basic purpose in any trial. We can be confident that God wants us to trust Him with faith which is "more precious than gold" (1 Peter 1:7).

At the end of the day we don't need explanations, we only need God. In fact, we need God more than we need explanations!

When David was in deep distress, he cried to the Lord for an explanation. He begins, "How long, O LORD? Will you forget me forever? How long will you hide your face from me?" But he concludes by saying, "But I have trusted in your steadfast love; my heart shall rejoice in your salvation. I will sing to the LORD, because he has dealt bountifully with me" (Psalm 13).

Notice the transition in this Psalm. David begins by asking for an explanation, and though he does not receive one word from God, he is satisfied by the time the Psalm is finished. He has not found a *purpose*; he has found a *Person*.

If God had given him an explanation, would he have been satisfied? No, because the distress of the heart is seldom cured by knowledge in the mind. God says, I will meet the needs of your heart even if you still have to live with questions in your head.

When the disciples brought news from John the Baptist that he was beginning to have doubts about Christ's messiahship, Christ said, in effect, "Blessed is the person who is not upset with the way I run my business" (see Matthew 11:1–6). Yes, blessed is the person who trusts God, even when God seems to work against us. For we can be confident that "all things work together for good to them that love God" (Romans 8:28, KJV) even if we don't see it in this life. God has all of eternity to prove that He had a plan that was best.

Blessed are the Jobs of this world who say, "Though he slay me, I will hope in him" (Job 13:15).